Fernando Rendón

月食中旅行

TRAVELING IN LUNAR ECLIPSE

BFH ACADEMIC PRESS

书名：月食中旅行
TITLE: TRAVELING IN LUNAR ECLIPSE

作者：费尔南多•伦东（哥伦比亚）

ENGLISH TRANSLATOR: LAURA CHALAR (URUGUAY)
英文翻译：劳拉•查拉尔（乌拉圭）
CHINESE TRNASLATORS：BAI SHUI (NEW ZEALAND)
中文翻译：白水（新西兰）
COVER DESIGN/ILLUSTRATION：SUE ZHU (NEW ZEALAND)
封面设计/插图：苏朱（新西兰）

ISBN 978-1-7386007-0-0

PUBLISHER: BFH ACADEMIC PRESS
E MAIL： bfhpress@outlook.com
BOOK SIZE： 6X9 INCHES
FIRST EDITION MAY 30, 2023

费尔南多•伦东 拉丁美洲诗歌杂志 Prometeo 的创始人和主任，麦德林国际诗歌节创始人和主席，WPM 世界诗歌运动总协调员，发表了《反历史》等多部诗集，曾获替代诺贝尔奖。

Fernando Rendón he is the founder and director of the Latin American Poetry magazine "Prometeo", the founder and chairman of the Medellin International Poetry Festival, the general coordinator of the WPM World Poetry Movement, he has published " Counterhistory " and other collections of poetry, he has been awarded the Alternative Nobel Prize.

记忆如露珠菌的菌丝一样弱不禁风
我们每天致力于铭记。

MEMORY WAS FRAGILE LIKE THE MYCELIUM OF THE
DEW FUNGUS.
EVERY DAY WE DEDICATED OURSELVES TO
REMEMBER.

～ Fernando Rendón 费尔南多•伦东

TABLE OF CONTENTS

BFH ACADEMIC PRESS

蓝奇屋学术出版社

反历史

如果奥德修斯放任任水手们对他的话充耳不闻
他会拒绝蜡和桅杆

他会在那女人无法抗拒的致命的歌声里
如鱼跳入水中，而生命了结

从而跨过这个世界王国的门槛
新的爱情之歌将在所有重要的基点迸发

我们凡人将怀着梦想孕育孩子
一批无形的勇士就会出现

最无情的暴君也会失去理智
听着重塑的鼓声，雷鸣咆哮

太阳和风将恢复
那些固执的盲人和聋哑人的神志

COUNTERHISTORY

If Odysseus had turned a deaf ear on the sailors
he would have rejected wax and mast

would have plunged in after the songs of
madness of those women ended like a fish

thus crossed the threshold of this world's
kingdom there would burst the song of new love in all c
ardinal points

we mortals would conceive children with
Dream a school of invisible warriors would arise

the most heartless tyrant would lose his mind
listening to the thunder of reinvented drums

the sun and the wind would give back their
senses to the self-willed blind and deaf

有人会从根本治愈森林的旧疾
在所有的纬度上
都能找到本能返回的路

啊，特洛伊，自我放逐
你的先哲被公开羞辱
凶猛的刀鱼
在你的逆滩上游荡！

someone would cure at the root the forest's old
plague in all latitudes the paths of instinct would be
found

Ah Troy, exiled from yourself,
your sages publicly shamed
and ferocious cutlass fishes prowling your iron
beaches!

和平鸽 DOVES

循环

玛格丽特发出一声惊恐的尖叫
当无意间，她纤细的脚陷进那个胶状的
以她名字呼唤她的沼泽。

近八个小时的无助里，她嚎叫着，怀里抱着一个
无形的婴孩。

下雨了，只有"地狱"这个词可以形容。

风和春，同行的陪审团，无声地谴责她的刽子手。

树木激增，愤愤不平着，又重新回到它们的根部。

痛苦蜿蜒而来，侵蚀着水岸。
远处：地球的年龄。

CIRCLE

The unwary Margarita gave a terrified scream
when her delicate foot sank into a gelatinous
swamp that called her by name.

For nearly eight endless hours she howled,
holding an invisible child in her arms.

It rained, and only the word *hell* could be made
out.

The wind and the spring, peer juries, silently
condemned her executioners.

Trees leaped, cursing, and then went back to
their roots.

Pain meandered, eroding the water's shores.

In the distance: the age of the earth.

茎梗刺痛了罂粟花的神经。
我们耐心抑或烦躁地
等待着。

被逼发疯的植物，我们迈不开步子—如在噩梦中
一样。

最大的努力后，我们勉强得以生存，处于人类荒
谬的最底层：捆紧发条的醉汉。

次日，饱经风霜的身躯，羽翼将更胜以往。

Nerves were stung by the poppies' stalks. And we waited between patience and impatience.

Maddened plants, we could not run – as in nightmares.

After the supreme effort, we barely held on to life, in the lowest rung of human ridiculousness: a clockwork drunkard.

On the next day, the battered body, the wings more vigorous than ever.

汇合

木头一样躺着，红色的树皮起皱，我们像是
在绿色的草地上行将腐烂的水牛。

却因为某种莫名其妙的随机举动，蘑菇一样躺在草地上，
我们探索了千年所有，逃离了史前的野兽，历经百战
数以万计的生命，永恒的拱门下
延伸，而魔鬼和渴望在云中战斗。

太阳在召唤我们，犹豫不决就是死亡。
飞吧，飞吧，美丽的天鹅，一切愿望会成真实现。

走在白露上，脱掉你的鞋子：
人类的年龄
不过是投向传说中的森林的刹那一瞥。

CONVERGENCE

Lying like logs, our red bark wrinkled, we are as buffaloes who rotting melt on the green meadow.

But due to an inexplicable random act, lying like mushrooms on the grass, we explore all the millennia, flee from prehistoric beasts, fight all the wars, are millions of beings stretching under the arc of eternity, while dragon and yearning fight in the clouds.

The sun calls us and to hesitate is to die. *Fly, fly, beauteous swan of desire, everything can be achieved.*

Walking on the white dew, remove your shoes: the age of man is that of his gaze upon the legendary forest.

记忆

不再是我的，而是我们的。

于我而言，我是一棵裸露着根部的光秃秃赤杨，在一年之初，一个世纪和一个千年之末，将种子吐入天空里厄律达努斯河水中。

在风中和大地中扎根的树，从森林走向湖泊，属于所有原始元素的盛宴。

我是声讨刽子手的树，饱受折磨的树，听着对所有年龄段伙伴的生长遗弃的诅咒，快乐渐逝，我兄弟们的希望被侵蚀，黑暗石器时代鸟儿的歌声，树液在萌芽中颤栗而出人类未曾见过的绿意。

对我来说，这棵赤杨生活在人类残害梦想、给感官套上紧身衣、让丛林的翅膀成为不真实的摆设的时代。

我说，赤扬就是一棵保护旅行者远行的桤木，根在光明之下。

MEMORY

*And there
will be no more mine, but ours*

Of me it may be said that I was an alder tree with naked roots, spitting seeds into the waters of the Erydanus river which flows in the sky, at a year's beginning, at a century and a millennium's close.

Tree that took root in the wind and in the earth, moved in the forest towards the lake, and belonged to the wild feast of all elements.

Of me it may be said, tree that cursed its executioners. And tree that suffered listening to the growth of abandonment's
curse on its fellows of all ages, the cutting-down of enjoyment, the eroding of hope in my brethren, the song of dark stone-age birds, the trembling of sap through the future of shoots as green as the human eye has not yet seen.

Of me it may be said, alder tree that lived in the era when man mutilated dream, put a straitjacket on senses, decreed the jungle's wings an unreal matter.

Of me it may be said, alder tree that sheltered travelers from themselves, its roots in the light.

空气

就像不愿落地的果实
宁愿在树上成熟到发臭的
被疯狂的樵夫砍掉

就像种子避开犁沟
或水牛昏昏欲睡不醒
在午后时分单调的固定模式里

是那些开先河的人
惊恐地从里面推开房门
当空气独自敲门时

随时登门造访任何人的空气
今天来了，明天不会返回
它们不请自来

因为，是种子啊！
地球上站起，拒绝死亡
自己解开自己的枷锁
终获永远的自由

AIR

Like fruits loath to fall
who would rather ripen until stench on a tree
about to felled by the crazy woodcutter

like seeds avoiding the furrow
or buffaloes eternizing their lethargy
in the monotonous herd at midday

are the men who with all their life-strength
in terror push the house gate from the inside
when it is only Air who would like to come in

Air   Air that visits anyone anytime
Air that comes today and doesn't return tomorrow
that comes uninvited

瞬间清醒
防止仅对自己一个人的任何外交
空气由远及近向我们发出警报和召唤
　　　　　　　　现在
严禁我们呼吸死亡
空气再次提醒人们，今天是个不存在的时间。
因为痛苦是永恒的
对享受的渴望
终不会成为礼物

an instant of lucidity in prudence
to prevent any diplomacy towards oneself

Air that alerts and calls from afar
                        and now from close by
forbidding the breathing of one's own death

Air that reminds one that today is the time which exists
notAnd that pain is timeless

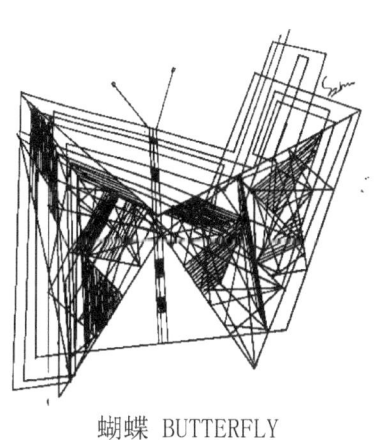

蝴蝶 BUTTERFLY

铁路

这是一首关于幽灵列车的诗。

一列消失在隧道黑暗入口的火车。

乘客尖叫着
当我们即将撞上一模一样的由同一个司机驾驶的列车
谁猛烈地将他的机车砸向我们。

蝙蝠盘旋在幽灵列车顶部，恐惧埋伏。

车身被黑暗笼罩，浓重得如前辈们的罪行，你忘记了铁路。

见证了早晨战胜死亡的感激之情，车队，在一个巨大的公园里，生活是靶场，过山车，提线木偶和家。

RAILWAY

This is the poem of the ghost train.

The train that vanishes into the tunnel's dark mouth.

Passengers of this train scream when we're about to crash
into an identical train, driven by the same driver, who
violently throws his locomotive against ours.

The ghost train over which bats are hovering, ambushed
by fear.

The train wrapped in darkness thick as the parents' crime,
the railway you don't remember.

The convoy that testified that the gratitude of morning
succeeded death, in a huge park where life is also a
shooting range, a roller coaster, string puppets and the
return home.

恩基杜使命

你们，克罗马努人，安全抵达我们沙漠时代的，不仅仅属于赫梯人的泥板，仍活在植物的精神中。

今天在笼子里，人和野兽蜂拥而至。拆除，然后，像以前一样，拆除陷阱的碎片，把沟渠填平。再冲进猎人们的庇护所，将湿气混入他们的火药，
折断他们匕首，染血的刀片。

来吧与牛群和鸟儿共饮，来吧在城市广场和田野上重吟那支让人想起时间之根的曲调。

我们之间变得不再简化，在没有乌鲁克压迫的独特的土地上，跨越界限，从你的目光中反射出丰沃的承诺、狂野的自由、尘世的血气，天界活力的权威统治。

TASKS OF ENKIDDU

You, Cro-Magnon safely arrived at our desert ages, do not belong only in Hittite clay tablets. Live still in the spirits of vegetation.

In the cages today men and beasts swarm around. Dismantle, then, as before, the pieces of the traps. Fill in the ditches. Storm the huntsmen's shelters to mix the dampness in their gunpowder and break their daggers' blood-dyed blades.

Come drink with the herds and the birds, come repeat in the market squares and the fields the tune that reminds one of time's root.

Be again irreducible among us, in a unique land without the oppression of Uruk. Leap over the boundaries, reflect in your gaze the fertile promise, the wild liberty, the full dominion of earthly vigor, of celestial vigor.

遗产

无人能把它据为己有。 属于任何人比某个人拥有更大化。而且，即便如此，每个人也必须先放弃它才能拥有。

凭借一种直觉，他们随后到达了新的隔间，这些隔间迄今已被围起来。

一位继承人显露贪婪或疏远自己时，一只狼蛛、一个意外的陷阱、一条蛇的嘎嘎声挡住了去路。 废墟上的满月。

一位身着锈迹斑斑盔甲的骑士，像只被腐蚀的铃铛，气喘吁吁地从海边赶来，他的剑在沙地上画出了危险区域和这一系列未知走廊的地图。

在记忆中，仍然沉没着一艘帆船、一种宗教、边疆和他们热衷于狂热的世界。

他们有最后的期限去发现一个中央房间，尽管时间很容易被拉长，就像他们的身体一样。 中央房间位于每个继承人体内，要进入它，他们必须破译一种藏在他们身体里的语言密码。

他们相继在深渊和拼杀撕咬之间放弃了一鳞半爪的宝藏。而下一个房间，不可预知。

LEGACY

No one can appropriate the treasure. To no one does it belong to a greater degree than to everyone. And, in spite of this, everyone must renounce it to possess it.

By a kind of intuition, they then reach new compartments, hitherto walled up.

A tarantula, a surprise trap, the rattle of a snake stands in the way when one of the heirs reveals his greed or distances himself. Full moon over the ruins.

A knight in rusty armor, pealing like a corroded bell, has arrived panting from the sea and with his sword has drawn on the sand the map of a hazardous region and of this succession of unknown corridors.

In memory there still sink a caravel, a religion, the frontiers and their world of virulent madness.

They have a deadline for discovering the central room, although time is liable to be stretched, like their bodies. The central room is in each heir, and to access it they must

decipher a language coded into their bodies. Successively they abandon a scale of treasures, between the abyss and the bite. And the next chamber is unpredictable.

神话

首先是他们的孤独，在发现理性和其他狩猎陷阱之前。

然后是边缘地带，荒凉的无辜，短发和难以捉摸的眼睛的人类，自古以来的争斗，他们砍伐了神秘的森林，使其成为一片荒地。

尽管如此，他们仍然在寻找。

他们找到了三叶草的小路，不屑于他们的过去，就像一个破败的庄园，目睹了消失的光景，遥远而缓慢的可能，疯狂梦想家的希望。

然而，沉船大海中的鲨鱼，千年尽头的悬崖，每个时代的旗帜下杀戮或死亡的必要，边界造成的幻觉，未修剪的杂草阻碍了树液，使感官变得迟钝，它们困惑的周期。

MYTH

First was their loneliness, before the invention of reason and other hunting traps.

Then limbo, barren virginity, the immemorial feud between short-haired and elusive-eyed humans, who felled the forest of mystery making a wasteland of its voice.

Still, they sought each other.

They found the clover path, disdained their past like a ruined estate, glimpsed the lost condition, the remote and slow possibility, illumination of ferocious dreamers.

There endured, however, the sharks in a sea of shipwrecks, the precipice at the end of the millennia, the imperative of killing or dying in the flags of every age, the hallucination created by boundaries, the unmowed weeds obstructing the sap, dulling the senses. They were cycles of bewilderment.

现在我们已经找到并认出了彼此，在巫师和天文学家的星空下发誓不再背弃命运，他们的辉煌让所有的阿尔戈英雄都变得苍白；我们拿着海蓝色的剑柄，面对美杜莎，自带敌视所有不公正的表情。

但在我们持续的奋进中，在走向传说的炼试之前，在榛子树荫下的池塘里，我们将洗净遐想，如微风拂过赤裸的身体，微妙而真实。

Now we have found and recognized each other, sworn never again to turn our backs on destiny under the stars of wizards and astronomers, whose splendor made all the argonauts go pale; we have taken the sword by its aquamarine hilt and facing the medusa, with the mien of one who despises injustice.

But before going to the high instance, to the legendary audition, in the hazelnut tree-shaded pond we shall wash the reverie, subtle and real as a breeze on naked bodies.

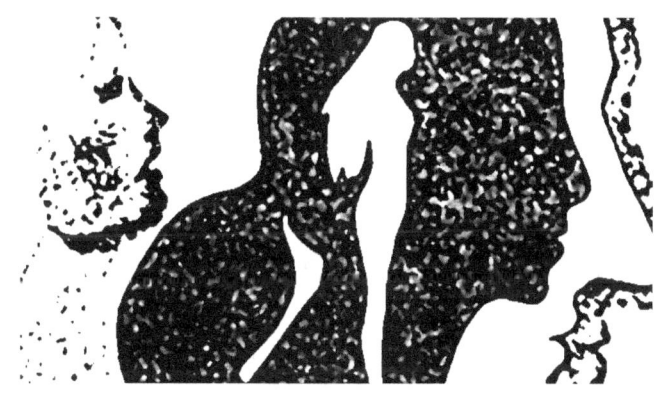

传说 MYTH

大船

撞上一片浮冰
它的船头断裂
从船厂到不知名的地方
时间之船来了

我领先而歌
船长睁大双眼
乘客惊慌失措，旅程不是旅游

明朗的夏天
倚在栏杆上
口哨里唱响了哪一首歌？

船上的甲板上我歌唱闪电
揭开整船老兵们苍白之面

我歌唱眼前的珊瑚礁
愚钝的无线电恐慌到端口
冰雹失措砸向船只右舷

但也有潜水艇的梦想
击穿日益增长的噩梦
执着的生命意志
平息飓风骤雨

VESSEL

Crashing against a procession of ice floes
its prow broken
from the shipyard to nowhere
there goes the ship of time

I sing the captain
his bulging eyes   insane
and the terrified passengers
because the journey is not tourism

And which song did we whistle
        leaning over the rails
                under the apparent summer?

I sing the lightning on board
uncovering the paleness
of the crew of veterans

And I sing the reefs in sight
the dumb radio   panic to port
under hail   panic to starboard

But also the submarine dreams
traversing the growing nightmare

The serene will of life
silencing the hurricane

树皮中的阅读

黄昏时分，独自从森林中走出。桤木的断枝察觉到。

但成熟是不能被骚扰的。

风将再次把露水撒进树叶的悲伤里。

沙漠将再次在空中与初恋相遇。

喜庆的夏日篝火，颤抖的爱的花瓣上蓝色的蜜蜂，
水晶之谜：你将对悬而未决的季节说什么？

READING IN THE BARK

At dusk, a being moves away from the forest. The alder's broken boughs notice.

But ripening cannot be harassed.

Again the winds will pour their dew on the foliage's sorrow.

Again the desert will be repopulated in aerial encounter with the beloved beginning.

Festive summer bonfire, bee of the blue on the petals of quivering love, crystal riddle: what will you say to the season in suspense?

嘉宾

主宾戴着围巾
一边咳着一边担心着
太多语无伦次的问题

每个人都向他表示祝贺
在公众面前他却承受着死亡的痛苦

面对众人的喧哗他哑口无言

脸色苍白，那是接近
死亡的面部
他们不停地拥抱他，围绕着他

没有谁愿意，被排除在
他的画面之外

THE GUEST OF HONOR

The guest of honor wears a scarf
and coughs, worried about
so many incoherent questions

Everybody congratulates him
while he suffers death throes in public

He loses his voice from so many thank-yous

And although his pale face
is that of death
they all hug him and surround him

And no one wants to be left
out of the picture

围绕写作

闪电以一种发光的、敏锐、严谨的方式写作。
一道闪电就是一个摩尔斯电码。
雨滴在墙壁上留痕。
风，在大漠的沙丘上标记。
太阳打在面颊。
河流淌过岩壁。
化石被蚀刻在古石的表面。
蜗牛在沙地上印出细长的光线。
啄木鸟啄着楔形文字的行话。

人们以缓慢的速度书写历史
用烟雾和灰烬来写虚荣
诗人是宇宙的读者。

AROUND WRITING

Lightning writes with a luminous, sharp rigor.
A flash of lightning is a Morse code.
Rain writes on the surface of walls.
Wind, on the desert's dunes.
The sun writes on faces.
The river on crags.
Fossils are etched onto the face of the ancient stone.
The snail prints a thread of light on the sand.
The woodpecker pecks a cuneiform jargon.

The people write history, albeit slowly.
Vanity writes with smoke and ashes.
Poets are just readers of the universe.

月食中旅行

故事从开始爆发就很激烈。并愈加疯狂。

黄色和绿色，滴落于城墙土壁，在柔和的阴影中。街头巷尾，洒下一片血红。

我告诉你"我们必须坚强"！

在你的手势比划中，大地喘吸。生命的浪潮注满一切，然后消失，世界变得枯燥乏味。虽说很长时间后，浪潮总会回来。

记忆如露珠菌的菌丝一样弱不禁风
我们每天致力于铭记。

原始的大地唤起我们与它的反叛运动保持一致。草地上的孩子们像天上的小马驹一样肆意奔跑。
当我们乘着太阳的战车，行星间穿梭，升腾降落时，这种骚动十足得狂野。

我看着文明在我眼前展开，却没能看到那些与我同道的人的面孔。

黑暗的死亡之神穿过身体来摧毁，并再次创造我们。在无限颤抖中我们毫不犹豫地释放自我，革新换面。

TRAVELING IN LUNAR ECLIPSE

The story erupted violently from the beginning. And it had gone mad.

Yellow and green, dripped on the walls of the cities, among the soft shadows. On streets and roads, a blood red spilled.

"We must be strong," I told you.

In your gesture, the earth breathed. A wave of life filled everything and disappeared, leaving the world dry. Although it took a long time, the wave always returned.

Memory was fragile like the mycelium of the dew fungus. Every day we dedicated ourselves to remember.

The original earth evoked us to align ourselves with its rebellious movement. Children on the meadow trotted like foals in celestial cycles.
Wild was this commotion, as we ascended and descended between planets on the chariot of the sun.

I watched civilizations unfold before my eyes, without seeing the faces of those who accompanied me.

时间如同生死一样强大。我被置于两者间，在两扇门前。

我们要做的，不是在顿悟一切之后死去。而是以完好的记忆和能量在不人道的户外环境中生存。

在黑暗而血腥的地球上，继续几个世纪的瓦解。即刻之后在仁慈而微笑的太阳的原子中自我重塑。

Time was strong as life and death. I was situated on both sides, in front of both doors.

What we had to do was not to die after having understood everything. To survive in the clarity of the inhuman outdoors with our memory intact and our energy.

To continue for centuries disintegrating among the dark and
bleeding earth. And an instant later to reconstitute ourselves in the atoms of a kind and smiling sun.

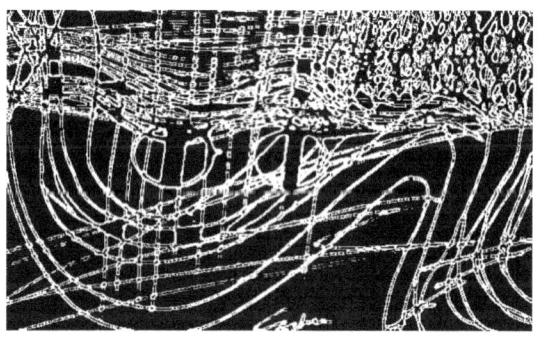

注视 GAZE

打开门

梦想
时空之源
世界的春天从这里诞生

复活的鸟儿被放飞
缝合我们的伤口

巨石
呼吸

磁铁
吸引音乐
没有人可以听
在不失去生命的情况下

传奇
打开大门

OPEN THE DOOR

Dream
source of the void
from which worlds spring

release the resurrection birds
close our wound

giant stone
breathe

magnet
attract the music
no one can listen to
without losing their lives

Legend
open the door

手网

一张手网铺就了世界的根基。 一张手网正在破坏他们。
宏伟的作品正在摇摇欲坠。

春天的热情召唤我们到野外的草地，因为阴影压在白昼的
边缘。

火灾和痛苦，但贪婪不会就此打住。
室外一切都变了，但人类痛苦依旧。

我们活着的，谁会否认：五官的河流一次又一次地流入感
知的海洋。

每天都有新的考验、严酷的事实流入睡眠之网，帮助化解
时间的粗重界限。

一张手掌，网定了世界基础，而另一张手之网，正在摧毁
它们。

A NET OF HANDS

A net of hands laid the foundations of the world. A net of hands undermines them. The magnificent work is crumbling.

The zeal of spring summons us to wild light meadows, for the shadow presses at the edge of day.

Fire and pain, but greed doesn't yield. Outside everything

changes, but man remains miserable.

We are alive, who will deny it: the rivers of the five senses once and again flow into the ocean of perception.

Each day new trials, hard truths, flowing into the web of sleep to help dissolve the coarse boundaries of time.

And a net of hands lays the foundations of the world, while another net of hands undermines them.

天空之旅

"诗人一口气写出一切"
（迪伦·托马斯）

时光短暂，奋斗永恒。
几个世纪的时间在一次心跳中被概括。
每个人的共同祖先们都在争论——
远没有在血脉上中达成秘密约定。
每个小时都用于决策。
瞬间，用于披露。
闪电温暖了户外。
我们醒来：梦想在它的元素中飘荡。
人群拥挤的气味中，我们是风的一部分——
而水是睡眠的一部分。
天空中的旅程。

THE JOURNEY IS IN THE ATMOSPHERE

"El poeta escribe todo de un solo aliento"
(Dylan Thomas)

Time is brief, the struggle eternal.
Centuries are summarized in a heartbeat.
Everyone's common ancestors argue –
and there is still no secret agreement in the blood.
Each hour is for decision.
The instant, for disclosure.
Lightning warms the sweet outdoors.
We wake: dream floats in its element.
In the smell of throng, we are also the wind's –
as water is sleep's.
The journey is in the atmosphere.

半梦半醒

　　　　　　　　　　　　　　　　当我死去的时候
　　　　　　　　　　　　　　　　便化青烟消失。

我梦见自己在做梦
你在我的梦中，眼里充满爱意
在你的梦中你清醒地望着我
在一个无法触摸的梦境里我们互视
一个持续的稠密的梦，包围所有
毫无疑问我们可以清晰地接吻
梦如大海
我梦见我们在海里相拥，说着荒唐有趣的事
这神奇之梦
可以伸展可以收缩，没有结局
许多不做梦的人，依靠做梦的人
一个人在明朗的日子里醒来并深爱，梦不会
停止对抗死亡，在半梦半醒中挣扎
如同磁铁吸引着时间的到来
因为不存在的东西才不会死亡

HALF-SLEEP

As I died,
I went up in smoke.

I dream that I'm dreaming
you're in my dream with your eyes full of love
you're awake watching me in your dream
we dream each other in a dream in which we cannot touch
a persistent, dense dream that envelops all
now it's clear that we can kiss
this dream is like the sea
I dream that we embrace in the sea and say absurd things
this dream has strange properties
it can stretch and shrink and cannot end
the lives of the many who don't dream depend on the
dreamers
one may only wake up and love in an open day without
ceasing to dream
live against death and struggle in half-sleep
attracting the time to come like a magnet
because only that which doesn't exist may not die

在我的梦中，静谧的不存在更加真实。
我知道这个梦必须被加强
我们有必要在无数个清醒的夜晚拥有梦境
最好是一个无边无际的梦，在这个梦里，世界
获得自由
每一秒钟都有一个梦想的浪潮
击碎你的现实，把死亡推倒
于是你第一次看到
自己活着

in my dream the serene non-existence is more real
I know this dream must be strengthened
it is necessary for us to stay awake many nights in dream
better a shoreless dream in which the world frees itself
each second a wave of dream brings down your reality
and brings down death
and you see yourself living for the first time

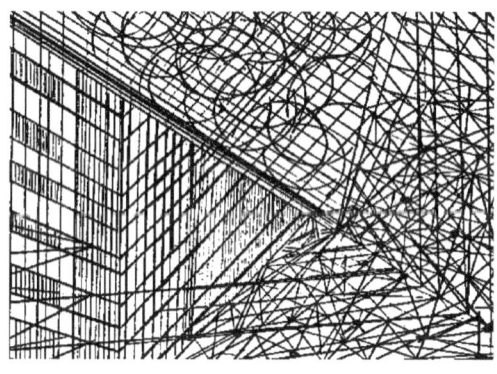

网 THE NET

北极之歌

我梦见自己居住在一个冰雪覆盖的地区，那里栖息着半裸
的人们。

我学会在冻结的墙壁上摸索行走，脆弱的小块
浮冰上摸索，不停地移动。

如果我停下来，冰块会在我的脚下崩塌，所以
我必须不停地移动。

每一步转瞬即逝间，我便发现时光的持续。

突然，一位女子驾着她蓝色的雪橇从这里经过，上
面坐满了孩子们。
他们歌声嘹亮。

ARCTIC SONG

I dream that I inhabit an icy region, where a semi-naked people dwell.

I learn to walk, groping at frozen walls, on a fragile sea of small ice floes, eternally moving.

If I stop, the ice gives way under my feet, and so I must move without stopping.

It is in the fleetingness of each step that I can discover duration.

Suddenly, a woman passes by in her sleigh of blue, full of children. And sings.

动物园

兽类是笼子

未来，毛毛虫一样靠近我们
它快乐并不急切
过去是一只打鼾的睡鼠，做着少而美丽的梦。
希望是一只白色的凤凰
我的渴望是一只猩红的羚羊，被国王的灰狗追逐。

这个动物园是笼子里的城市，每扇门上都有挂锁
目光所及，每扇窗户的栏杆上都有生锈的锁。

角落里，有否认与达尔文有关联的猿类
火眼的夜豹　像后悔坠入爱河般哭泣的鳄鱼
有主教胃口的蟒蛇　有诗意色彩的银行家
金刚鹦鹉　勉强做笑的鬣狗。

ZOO

The beast is the cage

The future comes to us like a caterpillar
 joy is not eager
The past is a dormouse that snores with few beautiful
dreams
Hope is a white phoenix
And my eagerness is a scarlet gazelle hunted down by the
king's greyhounds

This zoo is a city of cages in each door padlocks and
rusty locks in every window bars and eyes

In the corners apes that deny being related to Darwin
Night panthers with fire eyes crocodiles that cry as if
regretting falling in love boas with the appetite of bishops
and bankers
macaws with the colors of poetry hyenas that laugh
reluctantly

暮色渐重前，失去尊严的狮子和象形文字般的鬃毛 老虎
男人直视自己的眼睛 直视动物茫然的双眼
许多狱卒被铁链拴锁住

当你长大后，请帮助我们
打开所有的牢笼

给孩子们

before the tarnished day
lions that lose their dignity and their mane hieroglyphical
tigersmen looking into their eyes into the infinite eyes of
the animalsand many jailers chained to their irons

When you grow up help us open all the cages.
To the children

雄狮 A LION

诗的虚无

诗不存在
如果没有音乐呼唤你
抵达你
没有旋律让你的灵魂漫游

是不存在
如果没有音乐滋养你
触动你
没有足够的歌曲为你而存在
没有古老的曲调拥抱你
我所爱的，缺乏情歌的可怜人
没有遗产传给你
神灵们没有向你抛洒花朵的火焰
没有让整个宇宙的赤金降临于你
传奇音乐的金箔
风中树叶引人入胜的声音
构成了众生的宇宙，拥抱你
在所有时间的经纬间

我无声的爱人

THERE EXISTS NO POEM

There exists no poem
There is no music that calls you
That reaches you
There is no melody that makes your spirit travel

There exists no poem
There is no music that nourishes you
That touches you
There were not enough songs for you
No archaic song embraced you
My beloved poor in love songs
No inheritance fell to you
The gods didn't throw flower blazes at you
Didn't make all the universe's red gold descend on you
The gold of legendary music
All the inebriating sound of leaves in the wind
Making up the universe of beings that embrace you
In the warp and woof of all times

My songless beloved

水线上

我们是从人类灭亡的启示录中开始血腥的行军，伴随着战士们的呐喊声，在一个致命伤害了我们所有希望和欲望的恐慌的天空之下。

我们是何时放弃自己，将命运抛向兄弟的背后，疯狂地逃到谵妄边缘，在那里，地狱之城已不再可见。

我们是何时知道春天的大门会打开，但不仅仅为我们单独敞开，我们按时错过一直深爱着的人类的影子，从一开始就深爱着，当草原上还没有死亡，泥潭还未从人类的思想中涌出。

然后，再次回返，解开我们心中甜蜜而又累累伤痕的国家纠结，解开我们共同生活的跌落梦想的虚无，在水线之上。

ON WATERLINE

I

When did we begin our bloody march from the
Apocalypse
of Shadow of Man, among the cries of the warriors, under
a panic sky that mortally wounded all our hopes and
desires.

When did we renounce ourselves to throw our lot on the
brother's back, fleeing to the margins of delirium where
the cities of hell can no longer be seen.

When did we know that the doors of spring would open
and not open for us alone, that we would punctually miss
Shadow of Man, whom we had loved since the beginning,
when there was no death in the meadows in bloom and
the bogs had not yet issued from the human mind.

Again, then, to return, to undo in the heart the knot of our
sweet wounded country, the nothingness of our lost
dream of a life shared on waterline.

第二部分

鹦鹉的欢乐影子，
隐遁在树梢的阴影中，高谈阔论在猿猴的嘈杂之上。
树叶摇曳之舞在美洲豹的影子之上。
灼热的太阳是火蜥蜴唯一的庇护所。
缓缓匍匐于阴影上方的云影，潜伏阴影遮盖着恐惧阴影。
一个人的影子躲避着另一个人的影子。

到达的人们，海洋般的影子扑向那些已经不再了
的人的影子。
永远不眠、惊讶的人尖啸。
黑夜笼罩着光溪，流入人类影子的瞳孔，将阴影与光融为
一体。

II

The happy shadows of the macaws, sheltered in shadow in
the treetops, chatter above the racket of the apes'
shadows.
The shadow of the foliage dances above the shadow of the
jaguar. A violent sun is the salamander's only shelter.
Shadows of slow clouds over crouching shadows, stalking
shadows over fearful shadows. A man's shadow eludes
another man's shadow.

The arriving man's sea of shadows swoops down on the
shadow of the man who was. The always sleepless, the
astonished one ululates. It is night over the brook of light,
which flows into the pupil of Shadow of Man, joining
shadow to brightness.

第三部分

在沙漠中，
人类的影子对人有何意义？
一棵树的阴影比一个人更重。
在沙漠中，
中暑的阴影知道天堂是真正的阴凉处。

III

What use is his shadow in the desert to man?
A tree's shadow weighs more than a man's.
In the desert,
the shadow of the sunstroke knows that
paradise is a real shade.

欢乐影子 THE HAPPY SHADOWS

第四部分

"石头会尖叫"。

石头，选择王子的护身符，存在与起源的骨头，我认识你
神圣的灵魂。

我们的祖先在魔法的石头中挖掘，在咒语的石屋中进入，
那里无形的生命里诉说。

史前的日晷，影子环绕着石头，听着人类的心跳。

安菲翁的竖琴唤醒了底比斯漂浮的那里
石头。从石头中发出的声音沿着耳朵的迷宫传播。

从太阳石降临，并被阴影淹没，
人类不再倾听唱歌的石头。

IV

*"The stones
will scream".*

Stone, talisman that chose the princes, bone of presence
and beginning, I recognize your sacred spirit.

Our forebears dug in the stone of charms, entered the
stone house of spells, where invisible life speaks.

Prehistoric sundial, the shadow circles the stone, which
listens to the heartbeats of man.

Amphion's lyre roused the floating stones of Thebes.
Voices sprouting from the stone travel along the ear's
labyrinth.

Descended from the sun stone and flooded in shadow,
man no longer listens to the singing stone.

第五部分

石匠，他们揭示了固体的秘密转化，黎明脉冲
的新辐射，曾经被闪电寄居的石头之心，在光的
漂浮下，无岸之水涌现之前，锻造了花朵和动物的网，将
森林变为家园。

V

Lapidary, they reveal secret transformations of the solids, new emanations of the dawn's pulse, of the heart of stone once inhabited by lightning, before a shoreless water emerged under the floating light, forging a web of flowers and animals, to make a homeland out of the forest.

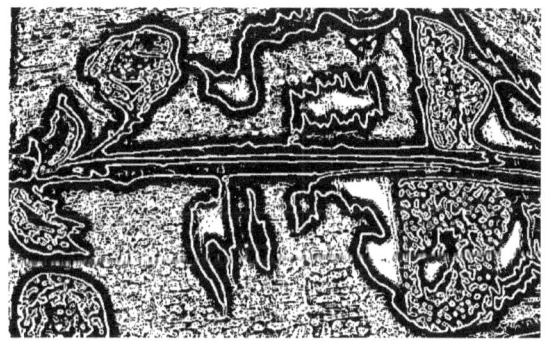

失乐园 PARADISE LOST

英译作者简介：

劳拉·查拉尔，1976 年出生于乌拉圭蒙得维的亚，
她曾接受律师培训。著有《忘却：诗歌》(Coal City
Press,2017)。她还出版了众多的西班牙语翻译作品（包括
简·奥斯汀和玛丽·沃尔斯通克拉夫特的作品），并著有儿童
文学作品。她的选集《触摸白昼之光：六位乌拉圭诗人》
于去年由 VelizBooks 出版。获得多个文学奖项，曾获得也
普什卡特奖的提名，她的第一本英文短篇小说集
即将出版。

ENGLISH TRANSLATOR：

Laura Chalar (b. 1976) was born in Montevideo, Uruguay,
where she trained as a lawyer. She is the author of six books,
most recently Unlearning: Poems (Coal City Press, 2017). She
has also published numerous translations from and into Spanish
(including works by Jane Austen and Mary Wollstonecraft), as
well as writing for children. Her anthology Touching the Light
of Day: Six Uruguayan Poets was published last year by Veliz
Books. The recipient of several literary awards, Laura is also a
Pushcart Prize nominee whose first short- story collection in
English is forthcoming。

中译者简介 :

白水，新西兰诗人，企业家，大洋洲 ASP 国际诗苑翻译。

CHINESE TRANSLATOR:

Bai Shui, is a poet, an entrepreneur, and a translator for the ASP All Souls Poetry Association.

插图作者简介 :

苏朱，新西兰诗人，艺术家，国际诗歌交流的推动者，WPM 世界诗歌运动亚洲协调员。

ILLUSTRATOR :

Sue Zhu, is a New Zealand Chinese Poet, Artist, Promoter of world modern poetry exchanges, and the continental coordinator of the World Poetry Movement (WPM).

和平鸽 PEACE DAVE

First Edition 2023
BFH ACADEMIC PRESS

www.ingramcontent.com/pod-product-compliance
Lightning Source LLC
Chambersburg PA
CBHW071144250626
47159CB00006B/2289